ROSY, RUBBER,
AND
SAND BOAS

R. D. Bartlett

BARRON'S

Acknowledgments

Many friends assisted me in numerous ways in the preparation of this book. Thanks go to Rob MacInnes, Chris Harrison, Bill Love, Chris McQuade, Rick Staub, E. J. Pirog, Brad Smith, Jim Melli, Brian Emanuel, Bruce Miller, Scott Miller, Dan Scolaro, R. Wayne Van Devender, and Karl Switak for their help, comments, and suggestions. Special thanks are due Randy and Krista Limburg for introducing us to, and keeping us familiar with, their beautiful albino rosy boas.

And as always, my sincere appreciation to my editor Anna Damaskos, for her suggestions and guidance.

Photo Credits

Dick Bartlett, Chris Harrison, Brad Smith, and R. Wayne Van Devender

© Copyright 2005 by Richard Bartlett

All inquiries should be addressed to:
Barron's Educational Series, Inc.
250 Wireless Boulevard
Hauppauge, NY 11788
http://www.barronseduc.com

Library of Congress Catalog Card No. 2004062437

ISBN-13: 978-0-7641-3200-1
ISBN-10: 0-7641-3200-8

Library of Congress Cataloging-in-Publication Data
Bartlett, Richard D., 1938–
    Rosy, rubber, and sand boas : facts & advice on care and breeding /
R.D. Bartlett.
        p. cm. — (Reptile and amphibian keeper's guides)
    Includes index.
    ISBN 0-7641-3200-8
    1. Boa constrictors as pets. 2. Boidae. II. Title.

SF459.S5B3755   2005
639.3'967–dc22   2004062437

Printed in China
9 8 7 6 5 4 3 2 1

Contents

Introduction

Rosy boas and East African sand boas are fast becoming two of America's favorite snake species. Although they may bite (especially as a feeding response), these snakes are easily handled, quite affordable, fairly small, and hardy and colorful—all desirable characteristics for a captive snake.

When handling the snakes, lift them gently and quickly at a point about midway on their bodies. If you approach them gingerly from above, they will often strike (rosy boas) or snap to the side (sand boas). If they are tightly restrained and prevented from advancing, they may also bite. Let them crawl from hand to hand. If the possibility of being bitten by one of these snakes is a deterrent to your handling them, you might wish to initially lift the snake on a small snake hook, then transfer it to your hand. When this is done gently, these snakes will seldom bite—unless your fingers happen to smell like mice. Then all bets are off. But with all of this said, the rosy, rubber, and sand boas do not enjoy being handled frequently. They will do better if treated as display animals and handled only when necessary.

Because there is a marked amount of variability in rosy boas, keepers have become almost fanatical about maintaining locale-specific breeding programs. Many hobbyists enjoy knowing which particular canyon their specimen hails from, and breeders take pride in offering coveted examples from remote, seldom-visited canyons.

Many erycine species are adult at 18 to 24 inches (46–60 cm) in length, and the largest among them seldom exceed 48 inches (1.2 m). Despite being heavy bodied, all are supple, strong constrictors. None are of brilliant coloration, but many do have highlights of buff, orange, or yellow against an otherwise sandy tan to brown ground color. The ventral plates are narrow and are concave on one desert-dwelling, sand-swimming species.

This desert rosy boa, photographed at the Arizona-Sonora Desert Museum, was found near Bagdad, Arizona.

The pink-on-brown coloration of the Cameroon burrowing boa is unique among erycines.

Although the origin of this rosy boa is unknown, the even edging of the stripes indicate that it is a desert subspecies.

Rosy boas and a few sand boas are now immensely popular with hobbyists. Of these most popular forms, albinos and other designer color morphs have been developed. It seems likely that as other species become more readily available to herpetoculturists, and are increasingly bred in captivity, they, too, will eventually be seen in designer colors.

Are rosy boas really rosy in coloration? Except for the belly-plate color of a few examples, no, they're not. Geographically this snake actually varies greatly in color. The Mexican rosy boa is dark chocolate brown and sandy cream, whereas the coastal form is often gunmetal gray with irregular brownish-red striping. Other races have a ground color of variable gray with precisely delineated russet to orange stripes.

Rubber boas derive their common name from the rubbery appearance of their creased skin.

A profile of the rough-scaled sand boa.

The name *sand boa* is actually less than precise, for although one or two species are true dwellers of shifting desert sands, many do not dwell voluntarily in such open, arid expanses. Rather, the greatest number of species of these interesting boas often live in somewhat less than yielding soils consisting of sand, rock, and gravel, or on stabilized steppes and grasslands where they preferentially use burrows of other reptiles and small mammals rather than dig their own.

What Are the Rosy, Rubber, and Sand Boas?

The family Boidae (the boas) is a predominantly tropical family of snakes. However, the several species of erycine boas (subfamily Erycinae) range from the tropics and subtropics northward into temperate climes of Europe, Asia, and North America.

Rosy, rubber, and sand boas are all small but stocky, predominantly terrestrial members of the family Boidae (subfamily Erycinae). Members of this group are frequently termed *erycines* or *erycine boas*. The genus *Charina* contains both the rosy and the rubber boas of North America, as well as a single African species, the Cameroon burrowing boa that was long thought to be a diminutive python. Without exception, the sand boas (genus *Eryx*) are Old World species.

As with many other taxa, the nomenclature of the erycine boas is unstable at the moment. Rosy boas were long contained in the genus *Lichanura*, rubber boas in the genus *Charina*, and the Cameroon burrowing boa in the genus *Calabaria*. It has recently been suggested that all of them should be combined in the genus *Charina*, and although this arrangement is not yet fully accepted, we have done so here. It has also been suggested that the southern rubber boa be elevated to species level and designated *C. umbratica*.

There is a tendency to again subdivide the genus *Eryx* (that has long contained all sand boas) into two genera, *Eryx* and *Gongylophis*. Additionally, the subgeneric name of *Pseudogongylophis* may be used for the Arabian sand boa. We have mentioned this where appropriate but have continued to contain all in the genus *Eryx*.

The rosy boa and the rubber boa are the only two erycine boas that are native to the United States. The Cameroon burrowing boa is a denizen of forested areas and humid savannas of tropical West Africa. Some Old World sand boas range as far northward as southern Russia.

Rubber and rosy boas produce small litters of live young. The Cameroon burrowing boa is an egg-layer. Similarly, both modes of reproduction are now known to occur in the sand boas.

Because it is more brilliantly and variably colored, the rosy boa is more popular with hobbyists than the rubber boa. Rosy boas are of robust build, and although the tail is short, it is tapered. Although most are substantially smaller, adult females (almost invariably the larger sex) of the larger subspecies of rosy boas have been recorded at lengths of up to 42 inches (107 cm).

Rosy Boas

The rosy boa is a snake of the arid grasslands, chaparral, scrub, desert, and semidesert habitats. It may be found well away from water sources, but seems most common where at least a little surface water is available. Look for it near the environs of desert springs, streams, and canyon seepages. Rosy boas may occur in suitable areas from sea level to above 4,000 feet (1,219 m) in elevation.

Coastal Rosy Boa

The coastal rosy boa, *Charina t. roseofusca* (cost, variable by color morph, ranges from $50 to $750), is found from southeastern California to northwestern Baja California. This subspecies tends to have striping with uneven, almost ragged, edges. The stripes may be of pale rose, deep tan, or orange against a ground color of gray. However, some examples may be anerythristic (lacking red color), have a gray to russet ground color, and lack all traces of stripes. Albinos and hypomelanistic examples of the coastal rosy boa are also well known. These are variably patterned, having sparse to moderate orange striping and speckling on an off-white ground color.

Desert Rosy Boa

The desert rosy boa, *C. t. gracia*, ($50–$750) occurs eastward from south central California to central western Arizona. Although it has an extensive overall range, the actual populations are often associated with aridland canyons, and many have developed characteristic colors. This beautiful snake has rather even-edged brown to russet stripes on a gray ground color. Arizona examples tend to be very richly colored.

Mid-Baja Rosy Boa

The mid-Baja rosy boa, *C. t. saslowi*, ($65–$150) of southern and central Baja California has well-defined, straight-edged, orange to russet stripes against a steel gray ground color. This is the form often referred to as *myriolepis* (an invalid species

This is a typical coastal rosy boa from near Los Angeles.

Whether albino (seen here) or of normal coloration, rosy boas are supple and powerful constrictors.

The desert rosy boas from the area near Barstow, California, are pretty and precisely marked.

name) by dealers and hobbyists. It is considered one of the most beautiful of the rosy boas and is in great demand by hobbyists.

Mexican Rosy Boa

The Mexican rosy boa, *C. t. trivirgata*, ($50–$150) appears in northwestern Sonora, Mexico, on the southern

The rosy boas from the mid-Baja region are very precisely marked. This is a mid-Baja rosy boa.

Baja Peninsula, on Isla Cedros, and in south central Arizona. Although it is the darkest of the four races, it is pleasantly colored and in demand. The chocolate to nearly black stripes have even edges and contrast strongly with the cream to pale tan ground color.

The various subspecies of the rosy boa intergrade readily and extensively where the ranges abut. One intergrade form occasionally available in the pet trade has broad light to dark brown stripes and is referred to erroneously as *L. t. intermedia*.

Captive Hardiness

In all but perpetually humid areas, rosy boas are wonderfully hardy little boas. However, in the deep (and perpetually humid) southeastern United States, or in fog belts elsewhere, unless their cage humidity is kept low, rosy boas may occasionally develop a regurgitation syndrome that is difficult to correct. Although proper husbandry (suitably warm temperature, low cage humidity, and prey of proper size) may correct this in its early stages, the snakes can weaken and die if left untreated. This malady is discussed further on page 39. Many records exist for rosy boas surviving captive life for more than fifteen years.

Rubber Boas

The little blunt-tailed rubber boa, *Charina bottae*, ($50–$100) may be found from sea level to over 9,000 feet in elevation. These snakes are cold-tolerant burrowers that occur in moist, humid habitats along the edges of meadows, fields, streams, woodlands, and evergreen forests beneath logs, bark, rocks, and debris.

Considerable numbers may sometimes be found behind bark or in rotting stumps that remain in logged areas. This boa may also be found beneath debris such as cardboard and roofing tins, as well as in the burrows of small mammals. Although adults are usually only 15 to 20 inches (38–50 cm) in length, examples up to 34 inches (86 cm) in length have been found.

Traditionally, rubber boas have been divided into three subspecies: the Pacific, the Rocky Mountain, and the southern. The latter, a protected form (now elevated to a full species status, *C. umbratica*, by some researchers) generally thought of as a dwarfed race, is restricted to the mountains of Southern California and may not be collected except by specific permit. Because of overlapping morphological characteristics, unless their origin is precisely known, attempting to assign rubber boas to a subspecies is often an exercise in both futility and frustration.

In coloration adult rubber boas are uniform brown to olive dorsally and cream or yellow ventrally. Juveniles are much more colorful than the adults, being orangish, pinkish, or tan dorsally and pink to yellow ventrally.

Rubber boas are placid to the point of actual docility. When startled, they respond by coiling into a ball with their heads protected in the center. They will remain in this position for long periods if necessary. When placed on the ground again, they will remain coiled until ascertaining that all is safe, then uncoil and slowly crawl away. Captive rubber boas become accustomed to gentle handling rather quickly. They

This desert rosy boa was from an area near Joshua Tree, California.

This is a captive-produced intergrade rosy boa occasionally offered in error as *L. t. intermedia*.

This neonate Mexican rosy boa is from southern Baja California Sur.

soon refuse to engage in the coiling and head-hiding techniques.

Captive Hardiness

Rubber boas are not adversely affected by humid conditions, but they can be stressed by overly hot temperatures. Temperatures of 65–70°F (18–21°C) at night and 70–78°F (21–26°C) during the day are ideal. A terrarium temperature gradient and a "hot spot" (a warmed basking area) add substantially to terrarium suitability.

Once induced to feed, rubber boas may be considered hardy snakes. Longevity of up to twelve years has been noted. Because they are small and neither overly active nor particularly territorial, a pair or even two

pairs of rubber boas can be maintained in a 15- or 20-gallon (57–76-L) terrarium. Although primarily terrestrial (even extensively fossorial), rubber boas can and do climb. They will often sit on elevated perches in the terrarium. A substrate of several inches of barely moistened mulch or peat, as well as numerous pieces of cork or pine bark beneath which the snakes may hide, is recommended. Some specimens enjoy coiling and soaking in their water bowl.

Cameroon Burrowing Boa

The Cameroon burrowing boa, *Charina reinhardtii* ($150), has long been referred to as the Cameroon burrowing python. Although many questions about this little snake's relationship to other boas remain to be resolved, at the moment it is resting (albeit uneasily) as the third species in the genus *Charina*. There is no other erycine quite like this snake in morphology. Its coloration of bright pink to brownish-pink markings against a ground color of variable (but usually rich) brown is unique. Its head is barely wider than the neck, and the neck is of almost the same diameter as the body. The tail is short and blunt.

When in a defensive posture, a rubber boa may elevate and writhe its blunt tail.

A portrait of a rubber boa.

This snake is a very secretive burrower amongst leaf litter and in loose, rich soils. The two to five eggs of this oviparous boa are comparatively huge and have an incubation duration of about two months. The hatchlings, in appearance very like the adults but with red markings, are well over a foot (30 cm) in length and large enough to easily eat small mice. Wild-collected examples of this tropical West African snake are occasionally available in the pet marketplace, and it is now being captive-bred on occasion as well. It is a powerful constrictor, and may secure and overpower several rodents in its coils simultaneously. Adults are 24 to 36 inches (60–91 cm) in length. High humidity does not adversely affect this erycine. In fact, it is preferred. Nighttime temperatures of about 70°F (21°C) and a daytime temperature of 85°F (29°C) or so (a few degrees higher for gravid females) are satisfactory. Again, provide a temperature gradient.

Some More Old World Erycines

Many of the Old World erycines are better adapted for burrowing than their American counterparts. Most of these snakes are aridland species, favoring dry, sandy savannas and fields, semidesert and desert "wastes," and steppes. Besides burrowing, the sand boas often seek refuge and repast in the burrows of small mammals and lizards. Of the ten or so species (authorities have never agreed on the number of species or subspecies), only about half a dozen are seen frequently in the European and American pet marketplaces.

Because of their small size, sand boas, in general, do well in rather small terraria. A 20-gallon (76-L) "long" terrarium is sufficiently large to house a pair, a trio, or even two pairs (male sand boas are usually not seriously territorial) of adults of almost any species. A fairly deep substrate of fine sand or dry mulch will provide a suitable habitat. A heating pad or a heat tape should be placed beneath one end

Although it stands out against some backgrounds (above), the Cameroon burrowing boa can be almost invisible when on damp earth and forest detritus.

Neonate brown sand boas are often beautifully colored.

This is a freshly imported, rather typically colored East African sand boa from Kenya.

of the terrarium. This will provide a thermal gradient from which the snakes can choose the most suitable substrate temperatures. A daytime temperature of 92–100°F (34–38°C) on the hot end is desirable. The cool end can be of "room temperature" (76–84°F [25–29°C]). Temperatures can be allowed to drop several degrees at night. Gravid female erycines should have the option of remaining warm around the clock.

East African Sand Boa

The East African sand boa (including the Kenyan and the dusky sand boas) is known scientifically as *Eryx colubrinus*. Varying by color morph, this boa sells for $40 to $750.

Adult females of this secretive arid-land and savanna snake may be slightly in excess of 30 inches (76 cm) in length. These sand boas can be a bit snappy, especially when a feeding response is involved.

Although variable, these pretty little boas have a ground color that varies from pale tan through buff to bright orange against which large, dark, dorsal blotches are quite evident. The belly is off-white to white and immaculate. The more southerly examples tend to be brighter. Some examples are overall reddish brown and lack all but the merest vestiges of contrasting markings. Posteriorly the scales are

very heavily keeled. The tail is conical.

Breeding occurs in the spring and early summer, and three to twenty-two rather large, live babies are born in the autumn. If kept sufficiently warm, the neonates usually accept newborn mice readily. The occasional neonate may prefer lizards rather than mice for its first meal(s). These hold-outs will soon switch to pinkies if the mice are scented with lizard odor.

The East African sand boa is a very robust and hardy species. They breed most reliably if gently cooled during the winter months.

Because they (like most sand boas) apparently metabolize much of their moisture requirements from their food animals, it is not necessary (or even desirable) for a water bowl to be continuously present. Daytime temperatures ranging from the mid-80s to the mid-90s (29–35°C) are ideal. A nighttime drop into the low 70s or high 60s (about 21°C) is entirely acceptable.

Dedicated captive-breeding programs have now produced amelanistics (lacking black pigment), anerythristics (lacking red color), and boas having irregular and unnatural patterns. A particularly colorful orange and brown phase is known as the Dodona phase, named for the Tanzanian valley in which it occurs.

Arabian Sand Boa

Still a comparative rarity in the pet trade, the little Arabian sand boa, *Eryx jayakeri* ($150), is a sand boa in every sense of the word. Females of this diminutive erycine are 14 to 17 inches (35.5–43 cm) in length, and males are smaller.

The Arabian sand boa became available in the late 1990s, and has been sporadically available since. This is literally a specialized swimmer in the smooth, fine, desert sands. The lower jaw is strongly countersunk to prevent sand from entering the snake's mouth, the belly is concave to provide the traction needed to move while burrowed, the turret-shaped eyes are dorsally oriented, and the rostral scale is greatly developed.

The Arabian sand boa is normally busily patterned in yellow or orange against black or gray (but melanistic specimens are well documented from the northern portions of the species' range). The belly is light and unpatterned. This is an egg-laying species, producing two to eight eggs that hatch after about two months of incubation. It has been bred only a few times in captivity. Hatchlings are said to accept lizards readily, but are less eager to accept pinky mice.

Rough-Scaled Sand Boa

The rough-scaled sand boa, *Eryx conicus* ($75–$200), is among the most commonly seen erycine species in American herpetoculture. The females are very stout and may exceed 30 inches (76 cm) in length. Males are much smaller.

This is a common snake in India, Pakistan, and adjacent countries. It also occurs on Sri Lanka. It is not a persistent burrower, but does often use the burrows of small mammals and other reptiles.

Three rows of large dark spots stand in bold relief against the tan, buff, gray, or yellowish ground color. The vertebral spots are particularly large and may fuse into a broad zigzag stripe. The head is grayish, largely

A profile of the Arabian sand boa.

Although this light-colored phase of the desert sand boa is often termed the desert morph, neonates of several colors may be born in the same litter. Photo by Chris Harrison.

As the brown sand boa grows, its pattern dulls.

unmarked dorsally, but bears prominent postorbital stripes. The tail is very short and abruptly conical. The tail of the male is proportionately broader and longer than that of the female.

This species has fairly small clutches (normally three to nine, sometimes more) of rather large young. The neonates will usually accept pinky mice even for their first meal. This very hardy and adaptable sand boa is now being captive-bred in increasing numbers. They thrive in a "normal" sand boa setup, but often require a period of winter hibernation

This is a large and well-acclimated adult brown sand boa.

to cycle reproductively. Captives may be bred annually, but it seems that a biennial breeding sequence is more normal in the wild.

Desert Sand Boa

Eryx miliaris ($150) is another of the larger sand boas. Adult females attain a length of about 30 inches (76 cm). The common name of *desert sand boa* has been coined for this snake. Desert sand boas are typically of a rather bland brown-on-tan coloration. They appear only occasionally in the American pet trade. Most recently a somewhat smaller, dark northern morph, referred to as the Russian sand boa or the black sand boa, has occasionally been available. It is known by the probably invalid subspecific name of *Eryx miliaris nogaiorum*. This boa ranges into the southern regions of the former USSR and abutting areas of adjacent countries, where it occurs on sandy, rocky steppes.

The Russian sand boa has an underlying pattern that is typical of *miliaris* but has an extensive suffusion of melanin that may all but obscure the details. The back is often much darker than the sides, but from a distance the entire snake may look dusky grayish black.

This hardy snake is reported to be a biennial breeder, having small clutches of moderately sized young. Neonates may be reluctant to start feeding on pinkies.

Smooth-Scaled Sand Boa

The two races of the smooth-scaled sand boa, *Eryx johni* ($100–$400), are the largest members of the genus. Besides the nominate form, the brown sand boa (*Eryx j. johni*), there is the western sand boa (*E. j. persicus*).

The adult size of the female is up to 4 feet (1.2 m) in length. As with other erycines, males are the smaller sex. This blunt-tailed, gentle, and secretive boa is found in India, Pakistan, Bangladesh, and Iran.

Adults of the nominate race are often dull to rich brown in coloration, but juveniles, and a comparatively few adults, may be broadly banded with russet and deep brown, or of an overall russet hue. Adults of the western subspecies tend to be of a brighter ground color, with russet or even orange predominating. For this latter the common name of *sunburst sand boa* has been coined. This species has a narrow head, a greatly enlarged, shovel-shaped rostral scale, and a bluntly rounded tail. It is a persistent burrower in loose but not necessarily sandy soils.

This interesting boa is now being bred with increasing frequency in captivity, and the litters typically number from two to eight neonates that are large enough at birth to accept a small mouse as prey. To be cycled for reproduction, *Eryx johni* requires a lengthy period of complete brumation. Except when in hibernation, this species enjoys temperatures that near 95°F (35°C) during the day but drop by about 10 degrees at night.

West African Sand Boa

The newest sand boa to appear in the American pet market is the tropical West African species, *Eryx muelleri*. It sells for about $100. Despite being available only about two years, this poorly known sand boa has already acquired an impressive array of common names. You may see it referred to as *Mueller's sand boa*, *Saharan sand boa*, or most recently the *West African sand boa*. Actually this newest name

seems to best fit the species. In coloration, this is an orange (or yellow) on brown snake. It looks much like *E. colubrinus*, but does not have prominently keeled scales on the tail and has a fleshy knob on its tail tip. Females attain a length of 20 to 25 inches (50-64 cm), and the males are 4 or 5 inches (10-12 cm) shorter. It has recently been learned that this is another of the oviparous (egg-laying) erycines. Apparently the female retains the eggs until embryonic development is well advanced. The single clutch of eggs reported hatched in only fourteen days. Hatchlings lacked an egg tooth.

Spotted Sand Boa

Although not particularly common in collections, *Eryx jaculus*, the *spotted sand boa* ($150), is one of the old-time hobbyist favorites. Dorsally, this small snake is a gray or tan to light brown sand boa with irregular darker brown markings. The belly is light in color and unmarked. Adult females top out at about 2 feet (60 cm). This and the Tartar sand boa, *E. tartaricus* (another rarely seen species that sells for about $150), are so similar in appearance to the desert sand boa, *E. miliaris*, that accurate identification can be difficult. This boa occurs in Europe, southwest Asia, and North Africa. It is associated with grasslands, croplands, beaches, or other such areas having loose soil (but not necessarily sand) into which it may burrow easily.

The Central Asian sand boa, *Eryx elegans*, the Somali sand boa, *E. somalicus*, and the Indian sand boa, *E. whitakeri* (once thought to be a hybrid between *E. conicus* and *E. johni* but now recognized as a valid species), are not currently available in the American pet trade.

Amelanism and Anerythism

Amelanism (albinism), the lack of normal pigmentation, is a well-known phenomenon in snakes and is eagerly sought by herpetoculturists. Amelanism is best known among the erycines in the rosy boa and the East African sand boa. Even without the phenomenon of pigment aberrancies, rosy boas are wonderfully variable both in color and pattern intensity. They have a devoted audience.

Amelanistic (we'll call them *albinos* from here on) rosy boas are magnificent creatures clad in scales of pearl-white and orange. Some have eyes of blazing red, whereas others with albinistic traits have dark eyes. Although they once cost thousands of dollars, prices have dropped substantially. Neonate albinos today (2005) cost between $200 and $500, depending on their lineage.

The neonate albino pictured here was produced by rosy boa breeder Randy Limburg (*rklimburg@msn.com*). Descendants of his albino female, collected in Riverside County, California, in 1993, are now intermingled in the rosy boas produced by many breeders. It was not until the late 1990s that albino rosy boas became generally available in the pet hobby.

This is a pretty adult spotted sand boa. Photo by R. Wayne Van Devender.

Albino rosy boas are not only coveted for their own intriguing traits, but are seen by breeders as a key that, if used properly, will unlock the door behind which many other genetic mutations lurk. Such things as snow phases that lack black and red pigments (actually produced in 2004) and other colors and patterns will be made possible. In each succeeding generation albinos themselves become a little more variable. In his 2004 breedings, Limburg produced a boa phase that is being termed a *paradox rosy boa.* Apparently this boa is mostly of albino appearance but has some patches of normal pigmentation. It will be interesting to follow the traits produced in rosy boa genetics as the paradox genes are incorporated into breeding programs.

This is a neonate albino coastal rosy boa.

A small percentage of the rosy boas in San Diego County, California, and Baja California are anerythristic. This term designates a lack of red pigment. Thus when adult these boas are an almost unrelieved gunmetal gray in coloration (neonates may have traces of a pattern). Despite this overall dullness of color, the rosy boas of this color are of great interest to herpetoculturists, primarily because of the genetics and color morphs that will eventually result when amelanistic boas are bred with them. It is now possible to genetically engineer designer colors such as the snow phase mentioned above, and hobbyists are striving to produce additional morphs.

Albino, anerythristic, and snow morph (and an occasional paradox morph) East African sand boas are also now readily available. As with the rosy boas, the prices of aberrant East African sand boas (still often referred to as *Kenyan sand boas*) has dropped drastically. Today, rather than the thousands of dollars these morphs commanded only a few years ago, they vary in price from $50 to $500.

Rosy Boas, Rubber Boas, and Sand Boas as Pets

Because they are small, attractive, hardy, interesting, easily handled, and affordable, and several species are readily available, erycine boas are becoming the favorites of hobbyists. Still, the acquisition of these snakes should be a matter of deliberate intent, not an impulse purchase. Before purchase, decide on the caging, learn the snake's preferred diet (and its availability), and determine whether you have sufficient time to devote to its care. Do you want just one as a pet, or do you want to try to breed the creatures? If the latter, learn how to determine the sexes (it's really not difficult). Learn about the possible necessity of cycling the snakes to enhance the possibility of breeding them. Talk with other hobbyists, with zookeepers, and with naturalists about the snakes. In other words, research, research, research.

Okay. Now that you've made an informed decision, all you have to do is find the snake(s) in question, right? Wrong! You not only must find the snake, but must still determine that it is in good health, that it is feeding readily, and that the potential dealer is trustworthy. All of this can be easier said than done, and your success with your new captive will depend largely on how you handle its acquisition.

This freshly imported desert sand boa is emaciated and desiccated. It is unlikely that it will acclimate to captivity.

Present in this group are an albino coastal rosy boa, a Mexican rosy boa from southern Baja California Sur, and two rosy boas from the mid-Baja region.

How to Choose a Healthy Erycine Boa

Before acquisition, it is important to know what the snake *should* look like in terms of weight, coloration, pattern, and so on. Look at live examples in zoos, nature centers, or in the wild, or at pictures in books or on the Internet.

If possible, inspect the animal for physical anomalies: malnourishment; scars; abnormal scales; encrustations near the mouth or nostrils; retained sheds; and to ascertain that it has clear, dry-looking eyes, free of any cloudiness (unless it is in shed) or swelling. Sometimes the brille (the modified scale that covers the eye) is retained during a bad shedding experience and can cause eye infections. Look for dry skin around the edges of the eyes or an eye that looks filmy. Look at the belly to make sure there

This is a pretty, well-acclimated adult Tartar sand boa. Photo by Chris Harrison.

are no burns, open sores, or blisters. The ventral scutes should not have yellowish or brownish edges. When snakes become malnourished, they develop longitudinal folds of loose skin along the sides, or the outlines of their ribs may be seen. Ill or malnourished animals should be avoided.

An erycine boa that is breathing with its mouth open or that has bubbles near the glottis or nostrils probably has a respiratory ailment. Snakes suffering from respiratory infections may raise the foreparts of their bodies and heads off the ground and remain in this position for prolonged periods of time. Specifically, look for abnormal behaviors such as body twitching

This gravid female rosy boa was from Mecca, California.

Note the small eyes and thick but tapering tail of this spotted sand boa. Photo by R. Wayne Van Devender.

17

The desert rosy boas around Bagdad, Arizona, have strongly contrasting patterns.

or an inability to crawl normally. Avoid any snakes that demonstrate any of the above symptoms!

Body twitching or rubbing the face and body against cage furniture may indicate mites. Mites are vectors of disease and must be immediately eradicated.

Ascertain that the snake is feeding properly, and if possible actually observe it eating. A feeding snake is usually a healthy snake.

If at all possible, have your veterinarian examine the animal before you purchase it, or at least immediately after you acquire it. Your vet will be better able to assess critical issues, such as appropriate hydration and weight and the presence of infectious stomatitis or cestodes (endoparasites). Additionally, if any other problems arise during the examination, your veterinarian will be able to initiate a proper treatment regimen.

Where to Acquire Rosy Boas, Rubber Boas, Cameroon Burrowing Boas, and Sand Boas

Below we mention a variety of sources where you may look for your

erycine boas. Make sure that when you acquire your snake you are in compliance with all federal, state, and local laws, including how it is transported. Ultimately, it will be your responsibility and not that of the seller.

Herp Expos

"Herp expos" have become mainstream. It seems that there is at least one expo somewhere in the United States and Europe almost every weekend. At these shows you have an opportunity not only to pick and choose the species in which you are interested, but to meet other interested and experienced keepers.

In addition to the more common species of erycine boas, relative rarities are occasionally found at these shows, and because of the great competition between dealers, prices are usually very fair.

Internet and Classified Ads

Today many reptile dealers offer their products via the cyberworld. By instructing your search engine to look for *reptile dealers* or a specific species, you can often locate many for sale (see Web addresses on page 45). Classified ads in reptile magazines are also a good source of these snakes. Again, buyer beware! You should know your dealer or at least the dealer's reputation.

Breeders

There are many private breeders of erycine boas. Many of them are striving to develop new color morphs or to be the first to offer a new species. Breeders advertise on the Internet or in *Reptile* magazine. Since captive-bred and -born/hatched rosy, rubber, and sand boas are usually healthier than wild-collected examples, breeders are often an ideal source from which to acquire your snake. Breeders usually go to great lengths to assure the quality of the animals they offer, and many have an intimate knowledge of the species they work with.

Shipping

Erycine boas may now be shipped in many ways. Door-to-door deliveries as well as airport-to-airport services are available. Shipping is not inexpensive, but it is fast and usually very reliable. It is best not to ship snakes during very hot or very cold weather, or during high-travel holiday seasons. Unless you know your dealer well, it will usually be necessary to pay for the snakes in advance. Many dealers insist on cashier's checks, money orders, credit cards, or payment on the Web by PayPal. Do not hesitate to ask your dealer about the method of payment required as well as the means or company by which the animal will be shipped, the level of service used, estimated cost (including packing and handling), and the dealer's policy on DOA (dead on arrival) animals in case an accident occurs. Many dealers will guarantee live arrival if you work within their guidelines.

Collecting Your Own Erycine Boas

In the United States, erycines appear only in the West. Should you visit or live in these states, you may choose to collect your own boa. Do so legally. Learn of and observe the various regulations (if any) that pertain to collecting these snakes. Hunt them, but do so with no adverse effect on the environment. It is illegal to collect endangered and threatened species without a specific license. Specific laws may pertain to the transportation of snakes across state lines. It is up to you to know all the legalities.

Searching for these snakes can be difficult and time intensive but can also be an enjoyable pastime. By educating yourself on the proper habitat requirements, activity patterns, and all-around natural history of the species in question, you will increase your chances of success.

This is an adult of the "super-black" phase of the Russian sand boa. Photo by Chris Harrison.

Caging

Terrariums and Cages

Those erycine boas that live in arid-land habitats thrive best if kept in warm, low-humidity desert terraria or in simple cages. Species such as the Cameroon burrowing boa and the rubber boa, both adapted to more humid habitats, will require greater cage humidity and a substrate somewhat different than that provided for the sand boas.

Both aridland and forest terraria are easily built and may be constructed at several levels of complexity. Simple cages are even easier, but certainly not as aesthetically pleasing.

Because erycines are secretive and inactive snakes, small cages seem

entirely suitable for them. For a pair, or even a trio, of most of the smaller species, a "long" (12 × 12 × 30 inches [30 cm × 30 cm × 76 cm]) cage or terrarium having a 20-gallon (76-L) volume would suffice. An adult pair or trio of smooth-scaled sand boas (adults of this species near 4 feet [1.2 m] in length) will live in seeming contentment in a 40-gallon (151-L) "low" terrarium (18 × 12 × 36 inches [46 cm × 30 cm × 91 cm]).

Whether you choose to use a terrarium or a cage, its entry must be tightly closed and locked. If the top is not held firmly in place, erycine boas—every one a talented and persistent escape artist—will do just that: escape. So adept are these snakes at finding ways to open a cage or terrarium that you will often be left wondering how it happened. And top-opening terraria are no more impervious to the efforts of these snakes than those with sliding front glass or nonscreened ventilation holes that are "just a tad too large." Always think security—absolute security.

Although the size of a tank/cage is easily agreed on, the kind of substrate and cage furniture is more debatable.

This is a very small part of Randy Limburg's rosy boa breeding project.

An albino coastal rosy boa is seen in this portrait.

Note the turreted eyes and elliptical pupils of the Arabian sand boa.

Sand or No Sand? What's in a Substrate?

When hobbyists think of enclosures for sand boas, they often think desert. And when desert terraria are thought of, hobbyists usually think first of vast expanses of dry sand. There are two things wrong with this preconceived notion.

First, most deserts are not merely vast expanses of dry sand. To be sure, by definition, deserts are dry, at least on the surface. But there are boulders and gravel, escarpments and fissures. There are scattered patches of vegetation, and there are animal communities. And there is always at least a bit of moisture at some depth beneath the sand's surface.

But second and most important, despite their common name, with few exceptions, expanses of sand are not the preferred habitat of sand boas. In fact, of the many species, only the Arabian sand boa is a confirmed desert dweller. This is not to say that

sand boas are never found in sandy habitats, but most are in no way restricted to such habitat. Erycine boas are secretive and well able to burrow in loose soils, but many choose to seek solace in the burrows of small mammals or other reptiles, or beneath surface rocks or debris. So what kind of terrarium substrate is best?

This depends on the species of erycine you are keeping and your outlook on caging. To be kept successfully in captivity, sand boas don't need either a sand substrate or a naturalistic terrarium. In fact, many very successful breeders suggest that because sand boas ingest the occasional grain

Profile of a Russian sand boa. Photo by Chris Harrison.

Mexican rosy boas range northward to the vicinity of Organ Pipe National Park in central southern Arizona.

of sand, sand or soil substrates may eventually lead to intestinal impactions in the snakes. These folks advocate a substrate of newspaper, paper towels, or aspen shavings, used in conjunction with one or more hide boxes, for the aridland boas. All of these artificial substrates will suffice and are easily changed or spot-cleaned when necessary. Many breeders also use plastic shoe, sweater, or blanket boxes with snap-on lids or on racks designed specifically to hold them rather than glass terraria or cages. The choice is yours, and the variations are

many. Tightly closed caging receptacles build up far too much internal humidity for sand boas, so if you use lidded plastic boxes, it will usually be necessary to drill or melt (with a soldering iron) several ventilation holes into the sides. Be certain that the holes are not large enough to allow the boas to escape.

However, with that said, we must mention that we advocate naturalistic terraria and have maintained and bred sand boas of several species for years on sand-soil substrates. We have never once had problems with gut impactions of any sort.

It just may be that not all sand is created equal. For example, the sharp silica play sand available in garden stores may not pass through a boa's intestinal tract as readily as smooth desert sand does. But again, we have used both without ill effects.

A profile of an adult brown sand boa. Note the enlarged, wedge-shaped rostral scale.

Randy Limburg produced this line of coastal albinos from a female found in Riverside County, California.

We usually provide our sand boas with 2 to 3 inches (5–8 cm) of a sand-soil mixture, plus cage furniture such as rocks and limbs. Place any heavy cage furniture, such as rocks and limbs, directly on the bottom of the tank and affix it in place. This is a particularly important step, for if these items are not secured, your boas are apt to burrow beneath them and be injured. Once the heavy furniture is in place, add the smooth-grained sand. If you choose to add drought-tolerant plants—spineless or nearly spineless cacti (*Astrophytum* among them) and succulents such as those of the genus *Haworthia*—the plants can be left right in their pots and sunk, pot and all, into the sand. Periodically watering these plants will provide a bit of humidity and temporary moistening of the sand, but if done in moderation, this should do no harm. Manzanita branches or cholla (cactus) skeletons can also be added.

Keep in mind that an arrangement such as this is heavy and requires a sturdy stand. Be sure to have the under-tank heater (this can provide

When frightened, rubber boas coil tightly. This grayish-green example is owned by Mitch Mulk.

the heated basking spot desirable for gravid female erycines) in place before adding the sand and furniture.

This beautiful coastal rosy boa was found late on a June night near Borrego Springs, California.

The origin of this Mexican rosy boa is unknown.

Although in the interest of lowering cage humidity you may choose to not always keep it filled, a water dish should be provided. Erycines readily use camouflaged hide boxes. And don't forget a locking or clip-on screen or wire top. An over-tank incandescent (full-spectrum is not necessary but will do no harm) light fixture and directed-beam heat bulb will complete the arrangement. The light will be needed for the plants if not for the boas.

Even if you decide against plants, a bit of periodic subsurface moisture may be beneficial. If you have several inches of sand, accomplishing this is simple. Merely push a hollow length of PVC through the sand to the bottom of the tank. Once it is in position, slowly (the keyword here is *slowly*) *trickle* the desired amount of water into the standpipe. The water will percolate along the bottom of the tank, dampening the bottommost layers of sand while leaving the upper layers

This dusky East African sand boa is now being bred by Brian Emanuel.

Profile of a Tartar sand boa.
Photo by Chris Harrison.

Often much darker in coloration, the desert sand boa from the northernmost part of the range is often referred to as the Russian sand boa.

perfectly dry. Your erycines can then choose the substrate moisture level best suited to them.

Rubber boas and Cameroon burrowing boas will do better on a slightly different substrate and with higher cage humidity. For these species cypress-bark mulch or aspen shavings seem the best artificial substrate, but naturalistic substrates of leaf litter (including among others such leaves as oak, maple, fir, and redwood) are also ideal. Cage humidity can be kept higher by using a larger water bowl and keeping it filled with fresh water at all times. Occasionally, the surface of the substrate may be misted gently, but it should never be actually wet through and through. Rubber boas will prefer a cooler temperature gradient (65°F [18°C] on the cool end, 85°F [29°C] on the hot end), but Cameroon burrowing boas enjoy the typical warm gradient sup-

plied to sand boas. In fact, gravid female burrowing boas will preferentially seek substrate having a temperature of 95–102°F (35–39°C).

Strive to keep your boas from ingesting sand or leaves by accident. Once acclimated, most erycines will accept their prey from long forceps if it is presented slowly. If the snake prefers to search out its own prey, place a prekilled rodent or lizard on a smooth, sand-free surface (a rock or a large plastic lid will serve adequately). If the snake happens to insist on live food, it will be on its own, but the chance of sand ingestion (and ultimate impaction) seems small.

Erycines may coil and bask atop the substrate in the morning as it is warming or in the evening as it is cooling, but will usually coil beneath cover or bury themselves beneath the surface of the substrate when temperatures are too warm or too cold. A substrate-surface temperature of 95–100°F (35–38°C) on the warm end of the tank will provide the needed heat. If the cool end of the tank is between 75°F and 85°F (24–29°C), the snakes will be able to thermoregulate successfully. Gravid females should always have the option of remaining warm.

Profile of a desert sand boa. Photo by Chris Harrison.

This sandy-colored desert sand boa is from the southern portion of the range.

Feeding and Watering

Although the erycines are usually among the easiest snakes to feed, there can always be a problematic or reluctant feeder. Despite being very effective wait-and-ambush predators, a captive erycine boa may be so intimidated by an active or aggressive prey rodent that it will not only refuse it, but may refuse future offerings of the same species. In the wild it is the snakes that determine when and how a prey item will be accepted. Put simply, if the boa is not hungry, it will not hunt. Should it need to, the snake can escape the proximity of the prey animal in a relative flash. In other words, "encounters of the feeding kind" are instigated by the snake, in territory known to it and from amidst camouflaging cover. This is very different from a captive snake being subjected to the frenzied scrambling of a rodent that is dropped unceremoniously into the snake's cage, often at the whim of the keeper.

If a live prey item runs across an erycine boa's body or if it happens to nip the snake, it is very likely that the snake will be sufficiently frightened to refrain from striking and killing the rodent. In fact, if the rodent chooses to go on the offensive, the stressed snake will often not even attempt to protect itself. Two typical responses by a frightened boa are an uncoordinated attempt to escape, and coiling tightly and hiding its head in the center of its coils. This all has to do with the natural versus the unnatural—the predator now feeling it has become the prey.

Rodents have impressive dentition that has evolved for chewing. It takes only a moment for a rat or mouse to disfigure a snake or to cause wounds that may lead to infection or death. A bite by the rodent on the mouth of the snake may lead to infectious stomatitis (mouth rot), or on the eye may lead to blindness.

The solution to all of these potential problems is, of course, to feed your snake prekilled prey, and to let the snake advise you of when it is hungry. A hungry boa will often prowl its cage or will, while coiled, closely follow movements (including those of its keeper) outside its cage.

Both rats and mice can be purchased either prekilled and frozen or alive. The frozen ones must be thoroughly thawed and warmed before being fed to the snake. If they are purchased alive, the prey animals should be killed before being offered to the snake.

Most erycines will readily eat a warmed, prekilled lab rodent offered slowly on long forceps. Tailor the size of the prey item being offered to the size of the snake you are feeding and learn the snake's prey preferences. Some boas may prefer mice, whereas others will preferentially choose rat pups. Most erycine boas will eat more readily at dusk or after dark than during daylight hours. You may often persuade reluctant feeders to eat by laying a warmed, prekilled rodent in the door of the snake's hide box, and then leaving. Putting the snake in a small covered deli cup with a freshly killed rodent may also induce feeding. It is important that the snake not be frightened first. It is also important that the snake not be able to escape from the feeding receptacle. It may take minutes or it may take hours, but when its surroundings are quiet, its cage is dark, and the snake is left to its own devices, it just may choose to eat.

An "oversized" meal may be regurgitated during digestion. This is especially true if the boa is startled, is subjected to fluctuating cage temperatures or very high humidity, or is ill. Provide a secure box in which your erycine may hide while digesting its meal. Small-sized meals cause less intestinal stress. It is usually better to feed your boa two or three small prey items than one large one. The prey animals offered should be smaller in diameter (or at least no larger) than the width of the snake's head.

A West African sand boa eats a prekilled lab mouse.

When not disturbed unduly, Cameroon burrowing boas thrive as captives. Many examples prefer rat pups as prey.

they have a tough time swallowing even a newly born mouse. They may accept small lizards or pinky parts for their first few meals. Initially, feed each snake only a single item at each offering and do not feed it again until the snake has digested the meal. Once you are sure that all is well, that its digestive system is working as it should, and that the snake is showing signs of growing, you may offer it a bit more food at each feeding. Again, smaller prey items are better than large ones.

Reluctant Feeders

It is not uncommon for neonate, wild-collected, or erycine boas in suboptimal condition to be reluctant to eat their first meal, especially if the meal smells different from their normally accepted prey items. In the wild, the neonates of many erycines prefer small lizards, a prey item than many hobbyists find difficult to provide. Remember, it is imperative that you induce your erycine to eat voluntarily. Once it is eating well, you can begin working on changing over to more readily available prey, such as small mice or rats. If you do offer your snake lizards, the possibility of endoparasite transference from prey to snake will be lessened if you first freeze the prey, then thaw it before offering it to the snake. Some boas that have steadfastly refused a lab mouse may eagerly accept a white-footed or a deer mouse. Scenting a pinky mouse with a frog or lizard may work, as may bait-and-switch techniques (arousing the snake's interest by first offering it a lizard and then switching to a pinky scented with lizard at the last minute). As a last resort offer live prey. As mentioned, once a snake has begun eating, its diet can be fine-tuned.

If a snake does regurgitate a meal, remove the prey, then clean and sterilize the cage immediately. Isolate the snake from the rest of your collection (in case the problem is infectious). Wait several days before offering the next meal. Then offer the boa only one very small mouse. If the snake regurgitates a second time, veterinary assessment and intervention may be necessary. Begin by having a fecal sample analyzed. In some cases, not even veterinary care will help the situation, and the animal will succumb to the problem.

It is imperative that your snake be comfortable in captivity before you attempt to feed it. Often, this is as simple as allowing it to quietly explore and adjust to its new surroundings before you offer any food. Cage furniture (especially a hide box) will usually hasten an erycine's acclimatizing. After an appropriate amount of time, food can be offered to the snake.

Many erycine boas will refuse food when they are preparing to shed their skin, a time when impaired vision and other temporary impairments renders them the most vulnerable to extraneous injury.

Neonate erycines of some of the smaller species may be so small that

Tease-Feeding

If, after exhausting all combinations of live and dead prey of all species, the snake still hasn't fed, try tease-feeding the snake. Erycine boas are often most receptive to this at dusk, when many are normally the most active. With a prekilled prey item (the prey that the snake species in question would be most likely to accept in the wild) try tapping it gently on the snout to make the snake angry enough to strike, and ideally, hold on to and eat the item. While attempting this, hold the item in very long forceps and move stealthily. There's a subtle difference that you will have to learn between making the snake striking-angry and intimidating it. If the prey item is dropped, wait a few minutes, then try again and, if necessary, again.

Force-Feeding

As a last resort, force-feeding may be necessary. Force-feeding is very traumatic to any snake, and if done incorrectly may actually hasten it's death. Never force-feed a snake getting ready to shed its skin. When force-feeding is to be used, it should be carefully performed by an experienced herpetoculturist.

Mexican rosy boas are the darkest of the subspecies.

Again, we strongly urge that all captive rosy, rubber, and sand boas be induced to eat prekilled prey items. Unless they are caged singly, we further urge that when being fed, the snakes be monitored carefully and, if possible, offered their individual prey from long forceps.

Watering Your Erycine Boas

Unlike many aridland snakes, erycines seem to readily recognize substrate-level bowls containing water as a drinking source. However, because it seems that most species metabolize much of their moisture needs from prey eaten, aridland species may not drink frequently. Water bowls can work for or against your caging preferences. A small bowl on the cool side of a cage will provide far less humidity than a large bowl set on the warm end of a cage above an under-tank heater.

Caution should be used with arid land-dwelling snakes that are accustomed to low humidity levels in their natural environments. Often just the presence of water bowls in their cages may elevate humidity levels unacceptably. This is especially so in areas such as the Gulf states or the Pacific fog belt where the relative humidity is perpetually high. Except for rubber boas and Cameroon burrowing boas that may always have water present, it may be best to offer water only every second or third day in places where humidity is a concern, and then for only a few hours. Provide the water at the time when the snakes are normally most active. In low-humidity regions a small bowl of water may be kept in the cage at all times.

Breeding

Depending on the species that you have, as well as the latitude and altitude from which the snakes came, breeding erycine boas may be quite straightforward or somewhat involved. Unless your female was gravid when you received her, both sexes must be present. Sex may be determined (on most species) by the fact that adult males are much smaller than adult females, by comparative tail length, by comparative size of the anal spurs (if these are present), by probing, or, if the snakes are babies, by hemipenial popping (see diagrams for the last three).

Let's discuss the size differential a bit. Males of many of the erycine boas are somewhat less than three-quarters (some are less than half!) of the length

This rosy boa from an unknown location has very narrow dark stripes.

and most are substantially less than half of the weight and girth of the adult female. In fact, an adult female rough-scaled sand boa or East African sand boa may be a very heavy-bodied 26 to 31 inches (66–79 cm) in length, whereas the male of both may be fully adult at a slender 14 to 16 inches (35–40 cm). Sexual dimorphism of most other species is equally well defined.

As mentioned earlier, erycine boas may produce either live young (most species) or eggs (three species). The duration of egg incubation for the three oviparous species—the West African sand boa, the Cameroon burrowing boa, and the Arabian sand boa—is curiously variable. Eggs of the West African sand boa have hatched in as few as fourteen days, whereas those of the other two species have taken about two months.

To breed successfully, erycine boas must usually be thoroughly acclimated to captivity. Thorough acclimatizing these snakes may actually take well over a year, and some wild-collected erycines have bred only after having been captive for four or five years. Captive-born or -hatched erycines acclimate much more quickly to new facilities than their wild-collected counterparts, but it still will take several years for a captive-produced

A small cloacal spur is visible on each side of the vent of this male East African sand boa.

neonate to attain breeding size. Genetic compatibility is also mandatory. To help assure this, it is best to acquire a pair of snakes from the same general location. Size, weight, and age also are important considerations. Male erycine boas may become sexually mature a year (or even more) earlier than the females.

The Arabian sand boa is relatively new to the pet trade, and is still uncommon in collections.

Even when sexually mature and of adequate body weight, some erycine boas may breed only every second or third year. Like most other reptiles, sexual maturity is at least partially dictated by size, but age figures into the equation as well. Although the growth (and hence the possibility of sexual maturity) of these snakes can be "pushed" by feeding the creatures often and much, this early adulthood is probably not in the best interest of the snake. A snake so pushed will not only usually produce a relatively small first clutch of babies, but there is often a higher than normal percentage of infertility and neonate abnormalities as well. In fact, these problems have been known to manifest themselves for several subsequent clutches. It seems far better to allow the snake to take the normally needed additional

year or two to attain breeding size. Does normal (slow) growth assure a greater percentage of viable babies when the boa is bred? Absolutely not—but it does seem to increase the odds that when babies are produced, they will be normal and healthy.

This neonate coastal rosy boa was found east of Los Angeles.

A Discussion of
Probing and "Popping"

External sexual characteristics are so well defined on most erycine boas that neither probing nor popping to determine sex is often needed. However, both of these methods are definitive rather than subjective. If either probing or popping are done improperly, they can injure the snake. For this reason, you should have an experienced hobbyist demonstrate these methods to you.

It is important that the probe be of the correct diameter for the size of the snake, and that the probing itself be done very gently. Sexing probes are available from many reptile specialty dealers. Females probe only two to four (rarely to five) subcaudal scales in depth, whereas males of most species probe five to ten scales deep. It is best if one person holds the snake immobile (especially if it is large) while a second person probes. The snake is held upside down, its tail bent slightly backward. The lubricated probe is then slid

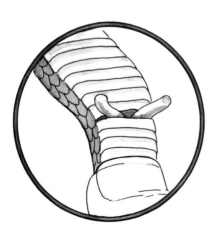

After carefully immobilizing a snake, the hemipenes of a male may be everted by applying gentle pressure and rolling your thumb anteriorly.

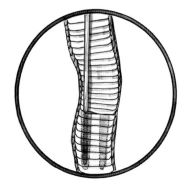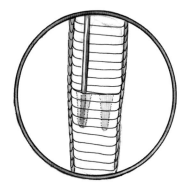

Gentle probing can determine the sex of snakes (male left, female right).

under the anal plate, pushed far to either side, and angled toward the tail tip.

A small opening (the inverted hemipenis if the snake is a male, a duct to a musk gland if the snake is a female) is present on each side. The probe is slid into this (which is why probe diameter is so important, lest injury to the snake occur) and pushed gently until resistance is felt. The depth of the insertion measured against the number of subcaudal scales is then noted and the probe is withdrawn.

"Popping" is a method of everting the hemipenes of newly born erycines. To accomplish this, it is first necessary to immobilize the snake while holding it gently upside down. Have one thumb immediately anterior to the vent and the other several subcaudal scales posterior to the vent. Bend the tail of the snake slightly upward (opening the vent slightly) while rolling the ball of the posteriormost thumb (the one on the tail) firmly but gently toward the vent. When this is done correctly, the tiny hemipenes of the male will be forced to evert through the vent. Females, of course, have no hemipenes.

Reproductive Cycling

Rosy boas and sand boas from the more tropical latitudes can usually be bred by merely lowering the winter nighttime temperature of the terrarium by several degrees while simultaneously reducing photoperiod and humidity. Some breeders prefer to cool only the male snakes, keeping the females warm throughout the year. Nighttime temperatures of 64–70°F (18–21°C) for eight weeks will usually suffice to cycle easier species (among these are East African sand boas and Mexican rosy boas).

However, most rosy boas, rubber boas, and sand boas from cooler latitudes or higher (hence cooler) elevations may require a complete hibernation for an eight-week period. This can be accomplished by cooling the snakes in a refrigerator to a temperature of 48–54°F (9–12°C). Before being hibernated (the new word for this is *brumated*) your snake must be allowed to empty its gut. Do not feed it for at least two weeks before placing it in the hibernaculum. However, the snake should be allowed to drink whenever it chooses. It is probably prudent to rouse your snake about halfway through its hibernation cycle and give it an opportunity to drink.

After the predetermined time has passed (again, about eight weeks is the usual period), increase the photoperiod, temperature, and relative humidity in the cage. This can be done gradually or in one fell swoop, as you prefer. After the boas are active again, feed them, place them together (if you keep them separately), and hope for the best.

During their winter dormancy, snakes of all kinds begin preparing for an ecdysis (shedding of the skin) that occurs a few days after springtime

This desert rosy boa is from Bagdad, Arizona.

This desert rosy boa is from an area near Kingman, Arizona.

activity has resumed. It is during and immediately after that post-hibernation shed that reproductively ready females produce the strongest stimulatory pheromones. It is then that males can be found following the pheromone trails of the females with the purposefulness of a trained hunting dog. In the wild, or if kept colonially, males may also indulge in stylized combat maneuvers, with the outcome being that the dominant male will breed with the female.

Because even a gentle nighttime cooling during the shortened days of winter may largely or entirely curtail an erycine boa's feeding desires, it is very important to have the snakes in excellent condition before lowering temperatures. The reluctance to eat may continue throughout the actual breeding season, even after temperatures have been returned to those normally provided in the summer.

It is while the snakes are seasonally quiescent that follicular development (in females) and gonadal recrudescence (in males) begins. It is thought by reptile physiologists that the inevitable parade of the seasons stimulates these reproductive system changes and ready the snakes for successful breeding when their period of activity resumes.

As demonstrated above, there are many cooling variables to consider. Interestingly (and inexplicably), this period of winter dormancy may be somewhat less important if the breeding stock has itself been captive-bred. There are also varying outlooks on whether to keep erycine boas together throughout the year or to introduce them only at breeding time. We have used both methods for several species and have found neither to work better

This albino female coastal rosy boa was found as a neonate in Riverside County, California.

than the other. However, if the snakes are maintained communally, the size difference between the sexes makes it necessary at feeding time to ensure that the larger snake does not engulf the smaller one. This can be easily accomplished by presenting the prey to each snake individually in forceps and watching until each snake swallows it fully.

Provide gravid female erycine boas with a temperature gradient. Although room temperature should be adequate for the cool end of the terrarium, a basking hot spot on the substrate surface of 90–98°F (32–37°C) is ideal. This will allow the gravid female to choose the temperature most suitable for the developing eggs or young. Improper cage temperatures can result in aborted undeveloped egg masses or partially developed or deformed young. Even a short period of improper temperature may result in aberrant patterns, scoliosis (spinal kinking), or other (usually unwanted) abnormalities.

Virtually nothing is known about the deposition sites chosen by females of oviparous erycines in the wild, but

A desert sand boa.

captive females will deposit their eggs in a receptacle containing barely dampened (not wet!) sphagnum moss. Such a container is often chosen by live-bearing species as well. A covered container, with an access hole of suitable diameter cut into one end, is usually more acceptable to the snake than an open-topped container.

After egg deposition is complete and the female sand boa has left the container, the entire deposition receptacle can be removed from the boa's cage. The eggs should not be turned on

their axis, but they should be removed from the sphagnum and placed in a closed container atop a substrate of damp (again, not wet) vermiculite or perlite in an incubator having a preset temperature of 82–84°F (28–29°C). (See page 45 for incubator sources.)

Check the temperature daily and add a little water to the incubating medium as needed. If possible, remove the eggs with obvious problems, such as fuzzy mold. If the eggs are infertile, they may show obvious signs of spoiling in one to several weeks.

Even after slitting their eggs in preparation for emergence ("pipping"), the baby sand boas may be in no hurry to leave. They may look out but remain inside the egg for as long as another day and a half. As they emerge from the eggs, they can be removed to another terrarium. Pinky mice should be offered after the post-hatching shed.

Like this East African sand boa, many species are strongly patterned dorsally and plain white ventrally.

Note the elliptical pupils of this East African sand boa.

Before acquiring your snakes, find a veterinarian who is familiar with, has the ability, and is willing to treat these creatures. Believe us when we say that not every veterinarian is qualified or willing. A veterinarian in your region may be found by going to the web site of the Association of Reptile and Amphibian Veterinarians.

As always, the starting point for assuring the good health of your boas begins with the basics. Start with a healthy snake. The next most important consideration is a proper regimen of husbandry.

It is always good, but not always possible, to see your snake before purchasing it. If you can't see the snake, such as when you buy from a dealer or individual online, it is good to know (or know the reputation of) your supplier. An online picture (in jpeg or tiff format) can help you get an idea of the color and body weight of the snake, but can actually give you little more information than that. It is up to you to inquire further. Ask if the snake you intend to purchase is feeding well on readily available foods and digesting the food properly. Ascertain that it is not retaining an old shed skin (or parts thereof, such

as eye caps), that it does not have a respiratory ailment, mites, or ticks, and is not overburdened with endoparasites.

Although it is better to purchase a captive-bred or -born boa than a wild-collected one, this is not always possible. Once you have determined as fully as possible that the snake is healthy and available, assess your facilities. The cage you are providing must be both escape-proof and suitable in every aspect to the inhabitant's well-being. The cage must provide sufficient space, adequate humidity (or lack of same), and a suitable temperature regimen. You must be able to provide a supply of fresh water and suitable food. Proper cage temperature and relative humidity are very important. All facets of proper caging for these snakes are discussed in detail in the caging chapter (pages 20–25).

This is a neonate coastal rosy boa from Borrego Springs, California.

Choosing Your Snake

When choosing your rosy, rubber, or sand boa, ascertain that

- the snake has no physical anomalies such as scars, encrustations near the mouth or nostrils, burns, swellings, open sores, or blisters;
- there are no retained sheds or retained eye caps;
- the ventral scutes do not have yellowish or brownish edges;
- the snake is not malnourished (there are no longitudinal folds of loose skin along the sides or the ribs may not be seen in outline);
- the boa is breathing normally (not with its mouth open) and there are no bubbles near the glottis or nostrils (snakes suffering from respiratory infections may raise the foreparts of their bodies and heads off the ground and remain in this position for prolonged periods of time);
- the snake does not twitch its body and is able to crawl normally;
- there are neither mites nor ticks.

Harcuvar Mountain rosys have rich burnt-orange stripes.

The origin of this desert rosy boa is the Harcuvar Mountains, in Arizona.

However, even with the best of care, health problems and concerns may occur. If caught in time, some health problems respond well to treatment, but others are irreversible, eventually fatal, and extremely communicable to other snakes. With the admonition once more that prevention is invariably better than cure, we mention some possible health problems here.

Quarantine

The importance of quarantining a newly acquired snake or one that has suddenly begun ailing cannot be overemphasized. Quarantine facilities should be in an area well separated from other snakes, and the quarantine period should be no fewer than thirty days (sixty to ninety days is better). The quarantine cage should be as sterile as possible, yet still appointed suitably to provide comfort for the snake. If more than one snake is acquired, each should be housed individually for now. During this period, observe your snake for any signs of respiratory distress or other symptoms of adverse

health. Discuss your findings with your veterinarian if applicable. This is, of course, an excellent time to have fresh fecal samples tested for endoparasites. Wash your hands and arms thoroughly before working with other snakes.

Regurgitation Syndrome

Improper husbandry, as well as illness, can cause erycines (and especially rosy boas) to regurgitate their meals when only partially digested or undigested. Excessive cage humidity and/or improper substrate temperatures are among the causative agents. Once begun, this can be very difficult to reverse, and it is potentially fatal. Prevention is the key to success. Keep cage humidity appropriate, and provide a thermal gradient within the proper parameters for the individual species.

This is a well-acclimated, adult female East African sand boa from Kenya.

This rubber boa is of very typical coloration.

External and Internal Parasites

Ticks and mites are external parasites that are bothersome but rather easily combated. Ticks are usually present only on imported snakes, but snake mites may be present in both imported and captive-born boas. The latter are very easily transported from vendor to vendor and cage to cage. Both of these parasites have been implicated in the transmission of very serious, often fatal diseases. Eradicating them quickly is mandatory. "No-pest strips," desiccants such as Sevin or DryDie, and spraying the snake and its enclosure with dilute Ivermectin are among the methods used. Several commercially prepared mite eradication products are also available, but we have had no practical experience with any of them. Follow the directions carefully and administer the spray sparingly near the snake's head. Once the snake has been treated, clean your cage, and any cage furniture, thoroughly and often. Wash all nooks and crannies and cage furnishings with a dilute Ivermectin solution or dilute bleach solution. Rinse the cage and furnishings thoroughly before reintroducing the snake to the cage. Be sure to wash and disinfect the holding cage in which the snake was placed while its permanent cage was being cleaned.

Initially thought to be a new species and called *Eryx rufescens,* this all-brown sand boa is now thought to be a color morph of the East African sand boa.

A profile of the West African sand boa.

Because most treatments destroy only the mites themselves (leaving their eggs still viable), it will be necessary to treat the snakes at least twice (perhaps even three times) at nine-day intervals to kill hatching mites. If infested with mites, your snake will often rub its face and body along a shelf or perch, twitch, or soak incessantly in its water bowl. Do not overlook these pests.

Internal parasites (endoparasites) such as cestodes and/or protozoa may be present. All are easily eradicated, but they do not all respond to the same treatment. We suggest that you consult your veterinarian if treatment becomes necessary. Administering medications orally will require physically restraining the snake.

Cryptosporidium ssp. are almost omnipresent, but seldom cause healthy reptiles distress. However, if your boa is stressed or its immune system becomes suppressed, cryptosporidia may proliferate and quickly debilitate the reptile further. A proliferation of cryptosporidia will cause a chronic, and often fatal, inability to digest food fully. If your boa begins to regurgitate frequently, seek veterinary assessment.

Trauma, Fungal, and Viral Diseases

Thermal burns from a malfunctioning hot rock or improperly baffled bulb or ceramic heater should never occur. Prevention is the best treatment. The primitive nervous system of a snake may allow these creatures to rest against a nonshielded lightbulb or an overheating hot rock, even while burning itself severely. Carefully shield all exposed lightbulbs or ceramic heating units with a wire net or cage (taking care that there are no sharp edges on which the snake can injure itself). Rather than hot rocks, use thermostatically controlled under-terrarium heaters to elevate the cage temperature. Should a burn occur, it should be dressed with an antibacterial burn ointment. Seek veterinary assessment if the burn is severe.

Rodent bites can be very serious. Although it is true that snakes are predators that usually successfully overcome their prey with no incident, this is not always the case. Prey animals have been known to seriously injure snakes in whose cages they have been left. Erycine boas will often not make any effort to overcome an aggressive prey animal. The snakes may even refuse that particular kind of prey in the future. If bitten by a rodent in the eye, blindness may

The West African sand boa is a relatively new addition to the American pet trade.

result. Mouth rot (infectious stomatitis) may develop from a bite or a scratch to the gums or mouth interior. Gaping wounds have been chewed into the sides of a snake by an unmonitored rat. We urge that all prey animals be prekilled or, if for some reason they are not, that they never be left unwatched in your boa's cage. If your snake is seriously bitten, dressing the wound with antibacterial powder may be necessary. If the bites are serious, immediately seek veterinary assessment.

Mouth rot (infectious stomatitis) can occur if a snake's teeth are broken or its mouth lining is injured. The medication of choice may be Neosporin or a liquid sulfa drug. We have found both sulfamethazine and sulfathiazole sodium to be effective. If mouth rot has advanced to the stage where the snake's jawbones are affected and its teeth are loosened, veterinary assistance should be sought. This is a disfiguring disease that can be fatal if not treated.

Respiratory ailments can occur if the temperature in your boa's cage is

A profile of the spotted sand boa.

suboptimal. This is especially true when the humidity is high or the cage is damp. Not all cases respond to the same antibiotic. Sensitivity tests must be done. Untreated respiratory ailments can quickly become debilitating and, if unchecked, eventually fatal. Seek veterinary assessment and help.

Blister syndrome (the causative agents of which can be many) would be better called *vesicular dermatitis*. It is an insidious disease that is difficult to cure, and can be fatal. It can occur if the cage is too humid (especially when the cage is very humid and suboptimally cool), when substrate remains too wet for a day or more (especially if the cage is both wet and dirty), or if your boa soaks for excessively long periods in its water bowl. Again, prevention is the best avenue of defense. Be sure the water in your snake's bowl is clean and that the snake does not soak continuously for more than half a day. If the snake persists in soaking, first check it for mites, then replace the bowl with a smaller one. Keep cage temperatures optimal. Prevent excessive humidity by providing adequate air flow and cage ventilation. Keep the substrate dry and clean. Should vesicular dermatitis occur, immediately assess and correct your regimen of husbandry and seek the help of a reptile-oriented veterinarian. If the serum-containing blisters are numerous or if skin damage is apparent, lesions may already be present on internal organs. Sensitivity tests are necessary, and antibiotic treatment will necessarily be lengthy.

Paramyxovirus is a very communicable, insidious, and eventually fatal viral affliction. As it advances, it causes spasms, loss of neuromotor control (especially noticeable in uncoordinated head motions), gaping, wheezing, and bloody mucus in the mouth. It has no known cure. This disease is highly contagious. The snake should be humanely euthanized. Know your supplier and quarantine all incoming snakes. Consult your veterinarian immediately.

Popeye is a condition in which the space between the eye and the brille may become filled with discolored serum. This may be caused by infection (often *Pseudomonas*) or injury to the eye or related ducts or other causes. Blindness or loss of the eye may result. Consult a veterinarian promptly.

Ecdysis (skin shedding): It is important that your snake shed fully at the proper time. A failed shed can lead to serious health issues. Improper shedding, such as retained eye caps, may occasionally occur if your boa is not properly hydrated or if the cage humidity is too low. As your boa prepares to shed, a slightly higher cage humidity may prevent potential problems. Check the shed skin to ascertain that the eye caps and tail tip have been shed. If it becomes necessary to physically assist in the shedding process, dampen the unshed skin slightly to render it pliable, and always remove the skin head to tail.

Glossary

Albino: Lacking black pigment.
Amelanistic: Lacking black pigment.
Anal plate: The large scute immediately anterior to the cloaca.
Anerythristic: Lacking red pigment.
Anterior: Toward the front.
Anus: The external opening of the cloaca; the vent.
Boid/Boidae: The family of snakes containing the boas and pythons.
Brille: The transparent "spectacle" covering the eyes of a snake.
Brumation: Often used to describe reptilian and amphibian hibernation.
Caudal: Pertaining to the tail.
cb/cb: Captive-bred, captive-born.
Cloaca: The common chamber into which digestive, urinary, and reproductive systems empty and which itself opens exteriorly through the vent or anus.
Cloacal spurs: The movable spur (remnants of a hind limb) found at each side of the vent.
Constrict: To wrap tightly in coils and squeeze.
Crepuscular: Active at dusk and/or dawn.
Deposition site: The spot chosen by the female to have young.
Dorsal: Pertaining to the back; upper surface.
Dorsolateral: Pertaining to the upper sides.
Dorsum: The upper surface.

Ectothermic: "Cold-blooded."
Endothermic: "Warm-blooded."
Erycine/erycine boa: Terms used to designate the boas of the subfamily Ericinae, the rosy, rubber, Cameroon burrowing, and sand boas.
Erythristic: A prevalence of red pigment.
Form: An identifiable species or subspecies.
Genus: A taxonomic classification of a group of species having similar characteristics. The genus falls between the next higher designation of *family* and the next lower designation of *species. Genera* is the plural of *genus*. The generic name is always capitalized when written.
Glottis: The opening of the windpipe.

Once a mainstay of the hobby, spotted sand boas are no longer commonly seen in the United States.

Gravid: The reptilian equivalent of mammalian pregnancy.

Hemipenes: The dual copulatory organs of male lizards and snakes.

Hemipenis: The singular form of *hemipenes*.

Herpetoculture: The captive breeding of reptiles and amphibians.

Herpetoculturist: One who practices herpetoculture.

Herpetologist: One who engages in herpetology.

Herpetology: The study (often scientifically oriented) of reptiles and amphibians.

Intergrade: Offspring resulting from the breeding of two contiguous subspecies.

Jacobson's organs: Highly enervated olfactory pits in the palates of snakes and lizards.

Juvenile: A young or immature specimen.

Labial: Pertaining to the lips.

Labial pit(s): Heat-sensory depressions on the lips of some boas.

Lateral: Pertaining to the side.

This very dark coastal rosy boa is from San Diego County, California. Photo by Brad Smith.

Melanism: A profusion of black pigment.

Mental: The scale at the tip of the lower lip.

Middorsal: Pertaining to the middle of the back.

Midventral: Pertaining to the center of the belly or abdomen.

Neonate: A newborn creature.

Nocturnal: Active at night.

Ocular stripe: A stripe on the side of the head that passes through the eye.

Ontogenetic: Age-related (color) changes.

Ovoviviparous: Bearing live young.

Photoperiod: The daily/seasonally variable length of the hours of daylight.

Postocular: To the rear of the eye.

Race: A subspecies.

Rostral: The (often modified) scale on the tip of the snout.

Scute: A large scale.

Species: A group of similar creatures that produce viable young when breeding. The taxonomic designation that falls beneath *genus* and above *subspecies*. Abbreviation, *sp.*

Subcaudal: Beneath the tail.

Subspecies: The subdivision of a species. A race that may differ slightly by color, size, scalation, or other criteria. Abbreviation, *ssp.*

Taxonomy: The science of classifying plants and animals.

Terrestrial: Land-dwelling.

Thermoregulate: To regulate (body) temperature by choosing a warmer or cooler environment.

Vent: The external opening of the cloaca; the anus.

Venter: The underside of a creature; the belly.

Ventral: Pertaining to the undersurface or belly.

Ventrolateral: Pertaining to the sides of the venter (belly).